FIND YOUR FLAME

CULTIVATING EVERLASTING MOTIVATION

J. Sakthivel

ISBN 979-8-89475-470-3

DISCLAIMER

Here is a disclaimer for the book "Find Your Flame: Cultivating Everlasting Motivation":

"Disclaimer: The content of this book is for general informational purposes only and should not be considered professional advice. The author and publisher are not responsible for any adverse consequences resulting from the application of the principles and strategies presented in this book. By reading this book, you acknowledge that:

- You are responsible for your own actions and decisions.
- The book's content may not be suitable for everyone, and you should consult a mental health professional if you have specific needs or concerns.
- The book is not a substitute for professional advice, therapy, or treatment.
- The author and publisher disclaim any liability for any damages or losses resulting from the use or application of the book's content.

By proceeding to read this book, you acknowledge that you have read, understood, and agreed to the terms of this disclaimer."

CONTENTS

FOREWORD

Find Your Flame Cultivating everlasting motivation has written by Mr.J. Sakthivel, a dedicated teacher in his profession and enthusiastic person in his speech and action, whenever we had a opportunity to share our thoughts he would always talk about positive attinide and self mouvanon. His finest interest is to spread and coach our younger generation to build their personality to inculcate the habit of self confidence self motivation and positive mind set.

Author of this book not easily taken this herculean task to write a book about Find Your Flame Cultivating everlasting motivation. He is a perfect person in the way he took proper coaching for self motivation and got encouragement by his coach to publish a book. His main inner drive is whatever he learnt from his experience and coaching, he wanted that same benefits should be given to readers of this book. To change the mindset of the people towards building a ordinary human being into an enthusiastic and highly motivated personality this book will be more beneficial.

A unique feature of this book author is to give the all motivational content in a nutshell way with vivid point of view that would definitely make an interest among young readers to read with more enthusiastically. All the ten chapters are very interesting and this book content is easily adoptable in day to day life. To improve a positive thought and motivating ourselves is a motive of the author. I am more confident that author's dedication, personal interest and motivation to publish this book would help the readers and mould the human mind as powerful one and helps lot to readers to overcome many challenges in many aspects of life.

Dr.R.Sivakumar

Associate Prof and HOD

Thiruvalluvar Govt. Arts College

Rasipuram TK, Namakkal Dt. Tamil Nadu.

INTRODUCTION

Have you ever started a project, hobby, or goal with lots of excitement, only to lose interest after a while? This happens to many people. The secret to staying excited and motivated is to ignite your passion. Passion is a strong feeling of enthusiasm or excitement for something. When you are passionate about something, you feel energized and eager to keep going, even when things get tough. But how do you find and keep that passion alive? Let's explore this secret to enduring motivation.

First, it's important to find what you love. Think about the activities that make you happy and excited. Maybe it's playing a sport, painting, writing stories, or helping others. These are clues to your passions. When you do something you love, it doesn't feel like work. It feels fun and rewarding. Start by trying different activities and paying attention to how they make you feel. This will help you discover what truly excites you.

Once you find your passion, set goals. Goals give you a direction to follow and something to work toward. They can be big or small. For example, if you love drawing, a small goal could be to draw for 15 minutes every day. A bigger goal might be to create your own comic book. Goals help you stay focused and give you a sense of accomplishment when you achieve them.

Another way to keep your passion alive is to learn and improve. When you get better at something, you feel more confident and proud of yourself. Take classes, read books, or watch videos to learn more about your passion. Practice regularly, and don't be afraid to make mistakes. Mistakes are part of learning and growing. The more you know and improve, the more exciting your passion becomes.

It's also helpful to surround yourself with supportive people. Friends, family, and mentors who encourage you can make a big difference. They can cheer you on, give you advice, and help you stay motivated. Join clubs or groups where you can meet others who share your passion. Being part of a community can make your journey more enjoyable and less lonely.

Sometimes, even when you're passionate about something, you might feel tired or frustrated. This is normal. Everyone has ups and downs. When this happens, take a break and do something relaxing. Rest is important to recharge your energy and creativity. Remember why you started in the first place. Think about the joy and satisfaction your passion brings you. This can help you stay motivated during tough times.

Lastly, celebrate your achievements, no matter how small. Recognizing your progress boosts your confidence and keeps you motivated to continue. Reward yourself for reaching your goals. Share your successes with others. Celebrating makes the journey fun and reminds you of how far you've come.

In summary, the secret to enduring motivation is to ignite your passion. Find what you love, set goals, keep learning, surround yourself with support, take breaks when needed, and celebrate your achievements. When you follow these steps, you'll find it easier to stay excited and motivated, no matter what challenges come your way. So, go ahead and ignite your passion the journey is worth it.

ACKNOWLEDGEMENTS

I would like to extend my deepest gratitude to several individuals whose support and guidance have been instrumental in the creation of this book.

First and foremost, I owe a profound debt of gratitude to my guide and guru, Dr. R. Sivakumar. Your wisdom, mentorship, and unwavering belief in me have been invaluable throughout this journey. Thank you for being a constant source of inspiration.

To my brother, A. Bharathi, your steadfast support and encouragement have given me the strength to persevere. I am grateful for your belief in me and your unwavering confidence in my abilities.

My sincere thanks go to my coach, Dr. Manjunath, whose expertise and motivation have been pivotal in shaping the concepts within these pages. Your guidance has been a driving force behind my work.

I am deeply thankful to my dear friends S.B. Viswanath, P. Pandian and R. Thirunavukkarasu, Your friendship, encouragement, and unwavering support have been a constant source of comfort and motivation. Thank you for always being there for me.

Special thanks to my diamond buddies, Saurav Das and Amith Kulkarni. Your camaraderie and belief in me have been truly inspiring. I am fortunate to have friends like you who have walked this path with me.

I am eternally grateful to my wife, K. Savitha, for her endless support, love, and patience. Your unwavering belief in me has been my anchor. To my son, S. S. Sugadepan, and my daughter,

S. S. Sugirdhana, you both are my greatest source of joy and motivation. Thank you for your love and for inspiring me every day.

Lastly, I thank my parents, whose love and guidance have shaped the person I am today. Your sacrifices and support have made everything possible. I dedicate this book to you with heartfelt gratitude.

Thank you all for your unwavering support and helping me find my flame. This book is a testament to your belief in me.

ABOUT THE AUTHOR

J. Sakthivel is a dedicated Political Science Teacher at the Government Higher Secondary School in Nadupatty, Salem, Tamil Nadu. He has been teaching for 15 years and loves helping his students learn and grow.

The author is passionate about personal development and motivation. He wrote this book, "Find Your Flame: Cultivating Everlasting Motivation," to help people stay motivated and achieve their goals. He has attended many personal development programs, including one with the famous speaker Brian Tracy, and has also participated in many one-day conferences.

In his book, J. Sakthivel shares simple and practical ideas to help readers stay motivated every day. When he is not teaching or writing, he enjoys spending time with his family, exploring nature, and practicing mindfulness. He believes that everyone has the potential to achieve great things with the right mindset and motivation.

J. Sakthivel hopes this book will inspire readers to find their inner flame and keep it burning brightly.

1. DISCOVERING YOUR PASSION

"Passion is energy. Feel the power that comes from focusing on what excites you"

– Opran Winfrey

Exploring Your Hobbies and Interests

Hobbies are crucial for unlocking motivation. Engaging in activities you love can reignite passion and creativity, providing a sense of purpose. Identifying and pursuing these interests allows you to discover new talents, build confidence, and find joy, fuelling your inner drive to achieve your goals.

Following Your Curiosity

Curiosity means things that make you wonder, excited. It's like going on a fun adventure to learn new things. When you let your curiosity lead, you discover amazing facts, new hobbies, and even new friends. Curiosity makes learning fun and keeps you motivated to explore.

Finding Joy in Everyday Activities

Looking for happiness in the small things you do daily. It can be enjoying a good meal, playing with your pet, or spending time with family. Smiling at little moments and being grateful for them can make each day feel special and more enjoyable.

Discovering What Makes You Unique

Everyone has special talents and qualities. Maybe you are great at drawing, telling stories, or helping others. Knowing what makes you special helps you feel confident and happy about whom you are.

Pursuing Activities That Energize

Doing things that make you feel excited and full of life. These can be hobbies, sports, or learning new skills. When you do activities you enjoy, you feel happier and more motivated. Find what makes you feel good and do it often to stay energized.

Chapter Summary

1. To find your purpose (or) your goal that make you become more passion

2. Curiosity makes you keep Learning every day

3. Celebrate your small achievements.

4. Identify your talents.

5. Stay with your purpose daily that will take you extra height.

2. SETTING EXCITING GOALS

**"Setting goals is the first step in turning
the invisible into the visible"**

– Tony Robbins

Creating a Vision Board

Making a collection of pictures and words that show your dreams and goals. Start by finding images and words in magazines or online that represent what you want to achieve. Cut them out and glue them onto a board or a large piece of paper. Arrange them in a way that looks nice and makes you feel excited. Your vision board should be placed somewhere you can see it every day. Looking at it regularly will remind you of your goals and keep you motivated to work towards them. It's a fun and creative way to plan your future.

Setting Goals That Align With Your Passion

Choosing goals that match what you love and care about. Start by thinking about what excites you and what you enjoy doing the most. Then, make goals that help you do more of these activities. For example, if you love painting, set a goal to create a new artwork every month. When your goals are connected to your passions, you will feel more motivated and happy while working towards them. It's important to follow your heart and focus on what truly matters to you, making your goals both exciting and meaningful.

Writing Down Your Goals

Putting your dreams and write your plans on paper. Start by thinking about what you want to achieve, like learning a new skill or saving money for something special. Write these goals in a notebook or on a piece of paper. Like "I want to read two books this month" or "I will practice the piano every day for 30 minutes." Seeing your goals written down helps you remember them and stay focused. You can look at your list often to remind yourself of what you want to achieve and track your progress.

Creating a Timeline for Achievement

- ⋏ Set a Goal (Day 1): Decide what you want to achieve. Write it down diary.

- ⋏ Make a Plan (Day 2-3): Break your goal into small steps. List the steps in order.

- ⋏ Start Small (Day 4-7): Begin with the first step. Do a little bit each day.

- ⋏ Stay Consistent (Week 2-4): Keep working on your steps regularly.

- ⅄ Check Progress (Week 5): Review what you've done so far. Make adjustments if needed.

- ⅄ Stay Motivated (Week 6-8): Reward yourself for small achievements.

- ⅄ Achieve Your Goal (Week 9-10): Complete all the steps and reach your goal. Celebrate your success! Creating a Timeline for Achievement

Sharing Your Goals with a Friend or Family Member

It can provide motivation and support. When you tell someone you trust about your plans, they can offer encouragement, advice, and hold you accountable. This makes it easier to stay committed and overcome obstacles. Plus, discussing your goals can help clarify your own thinking and inspire new ideas. Whether it's a career aspiration, fitness target, or personal project, involving others can turn your journey into a shared experience, more success achievable and enjoyable. So, don't hesitate to share your ambitions with those who care about you.

Chapter Summary

1. Looking your vision board regularly will remind you towards goal.

2. Goal set on your inner desire of own it keep motivates to you working towards your goal.

3. Write your goals in your notebook (or) paper.

4. Prepare action plan to achieve your goal.

5. Declare your goal to your family friends, neighbours. They will motivate you towards your goal.

3. OVERCOMING OBSTACLES WITH GRIT

Developing a Growth Mindset

Believing you can get better at things through hard work and practice. Instead of thinking you're just naturally good or bad at something, you understand that effort and learning make you smarter. If you make mistakes, you see them as chances to learn, not failures. It's important to keep trying even when things are tough. Saying "I can do this yet" is better than "I can't do this." Always try to learn from feedback and never give up. With a growth mindset, you can achieve great things by always working to improve.

Finding Inspiration in Stories of Resilience

Inspiration show us that people can overcome tough times with courage and determination.

For example, Malala Yousafzai continued to fight for girls' education even after being attacked. Helen Keller learned to communicate despite being blind and deaf. Thomas Alva Edison kept trying many times before inventing the light bulb. These stories teach us to keep going even when things get hard. They inspire us to stay strong, believe in ourselves, and never give up. Resilience means bouncing back from challenges, and these examples remind us that we can achieve great things if we keep trying.

Using Affirmations to Stay Positive

Telling yourself good things every day. Affirmations are like little reminders that help you feel happy and strong. When you wake up in the morning, try saying things like, "I am smart," "I am brave," "I can do hard things," or "Today will be a great day." These words can make you feel good inside.

When you say positive things to yourself, you start to believe them. This can help you do better in school, make new friends, and feel happier. If something goes wrong, you can use affirmations to cheer yourself up. For example, if you don't do well on a test, you can say, "I will try my best next time," or "I am learning and growing."

Affirmations are also helpful when you feel nervous or scared. If you have to speak in front of the class, you can say, "I am confident," or "I can do this." These words give you courage and help you stay calm.

Try to make a habit of saying affirmations every day. You can say them in front of a mirror, write them in a journal, or even draw pictures of them. Remember, positive words have power. They can help you feel strong, happy, and ready to face any challenge.

Seeking Guidance From a Mentor

Setting goals with the help of a mentor is like having a guide on a big adventure. A mentor is someone who is experienced and can give you advice. Here is how you can set goals with your mentor:

- ▲ Talk About Your Dreams: Share what you want to achieve. It could be anything, like getting better at math or learning to play the guitar.

- ▲ Break It Down: Your mentor will help you break your big goal into smaller, easier steps. For example, if you want to be better at math, start with practicing addition and subtraction.

- ▲ Make A Plan: Together, you and your mentor will make a plan. This plan will have all the steps you need to follow to reach your goal.

- ▲ Set A Time: Decide how long each step will take. It's like making a schedule for your goals.

- ▲ Check Progress: Regularly meet with your mentor to see how you are doing. If you face any problems, your mentor can help you to solve them.

- ▲ Stay Positive: Your mentor will encourage you and help you stay motivated, even if things get tough.

Remember, setting goals with a mentor makes the journey to success more fun and easier to manage.

Celebrating Your Progress Along the Way

As you journey towards your goals, it's important to celebrate the steps you take along the way. Each little achievement adds up to big progress whether it's finishing a book, solving a tricky math problem, or learning a new skill, take a moment to pat yourself on the back. Celebrating your progress helps keep you motivated and reminds you how far you've come. So, don't forget to cheer for yourself, maybe with a happy dance keep up the great work, and remember, every step forward is something to be proud of.

Chapter Summary

1. The growth mindset, you can achieve great things by always working, to improve

2. Keep aside inspiration stories that gives motivation to work harder.

3. Try to make a benefit of saying affirmation every day.

4. A Mentor is someone who is experienced and can give you advice.

5. Celebrate your progress every day. It will keep motivates your work more.

4. FINDING INSPIRATION EVERYWHERE

Keeping a Journal of Things That Inspire You

Journal is the treasure map for your imagination. Imagine journal is a special book where you write down all the things that make you feel excited, curious, or happy. Maybe it's a beautiful sunset, a funny joke, or a story that makes you think. Sometimes it's the little things, like a kind word from a friend or a new idea that pops into your head. By writing down what inspires you, you're capturing moments of magic that you can revisit whenever you need a boost. It's a bit like collecting shiny pebbles on the beach, each one a tiny spark of inspiration. So, grab your journal and start filling it with the things that make your heart sing Remember, inspiration is everywhere, waiting for you to discover it.

Surrounding Yourself with Art and Creativity

By filling your space with paintings, sculptures, and other forms of artistic expression, you invite beauty and innovation into your daily life. Creativity knows no bounds, and by immersing yourself in a creative environment, you open yourself to endless possibilities. From doodling in a sketchbook to experimenting with new techniques, expressing yourself artistically fosters personal growth and self-discovery. Embrace the opportunity to explore different mediums and styles, allowing your creativity to flow freely. Whether you're a seasoned artist or just beginning your creative journey, surrounding yourself with art can ignite passion and ignite a sense of wonder. So, fill your surroundings with art, and let your imagination soar.

Listening to Uplifting Music or Podcasts

Listening music mood can significantly boost your mood and motivation. Whether it's catchy inspiring talks, they have the power to lift your spirits and help you stay focused. By immersing yourself in positive content, you can reduce stress and anxiety, making it easier to tackle your daily tasks. Uplifting music or podcasts can provide a sense of encouragement, reminding you that you're capable of overcoming challenges.

Taking Walks in Nature

You see trees, flowers, and animals. The air smells fresh. Birds sing songs. You might find rocks or sticks. Walking is good exercise too. It makes you strong and healthy. Nature is beautiful. You can relax and enjoy it. It's a great way to spend time with family and friends. So, put on your shoes and go outside. Take a walk in nature. You'll have a great time.

Engaging in Creative Activities like Drawing or Writing

Children to express their imagination and explore their creativity freely. Drawing colourful pictures helps them visualize their ideas, while writing allows them to exciting tales about adventurous journeys or brave heroes. These activities not only entertain but also foster critical thinking, problem-solving skills, and communication abilities. By encouraging children to engage in creative pursuits, we empower them to think outside the box, discover new perspectives, and unleash their full potential as imaginative beings, shaping a brighter and more colourful future for themselves and others.

Chapter Summary

1. Writing down what inspires you. It makes you feel excited and happy.

2. Surrounding yourself with art can ignite passion and sense of wonder.

3. Listing music can boost your mood and motivation

4. Walking towards nature. We get fresh air, relaxed, calm, mindset, make you feel better.

5. By encouraging children, drawing, writing, visualize their ideas they develop new skills.

5. CULTIVATING A POSITIVE MINDSET

"Your positive action combined with positive thinking results in success"

– Shiv Khera

Practicing Positive Self-Talk

Self - talk can be a great way to help you feel happier and more confident. Positive self - talk means saying good things to yourself. It's like being your own cheerleader. Here are some ways you can practice positive self-talk. First, start your day with a smile and a positive thought. When you wake up, tell yourself, "Today is going to be a good day." This can help to set a happy tone for the rest of your day. Even if things don't go perfectly, remembering that you started with a positive thought can help keep you in a good mood.

When you look in the mirror, say something nice about yourself. You could say, "I am smart," "I am kind," or

"I am good at math." These positive statements are called affirmations. Affirmations can help you feel good about who you are. If you make a mistake, don't be too hard on yourself. Everyone makes mistakes. Instead of saying, "I can't do anything right," try saying, "I'll do better next time." This helps you learn from your mistakes without feeling bad about yourself.

Think about the things you are good at. Maybe you are good in drawing, playing soccer, or helping your friends. Remind yourself of these skills by saying, "I am a good artist," or "I am a helpful friend." This can boost your confidence. If you feel nervous or scared, talk to yourself in a kind way. Say, "It's okay to feel nervous. I can handle this." This can make you feel calmer and more in control. When you finish a task, even a small one, give yourself a pat on the back. You can say, "I did a good job," or "I worked hard on this." Celebrating your successes, no matter how small, can make you feel proud.

Surround yourself with positive people. Friends who say nice things and encourage you can help you feel better about yourself. When you hear positive words from others, it can be easier to say positive things to yourself. If you have a big goal, break it into smaller steps. Each time you complete a step; tell yourself, "I am making progress." This can help you stay motivated and keep going. Remember to be patient with yourself. Learning new things and building good habits takes time. If you find it hard to always use positive self-talk, don't give up. Keep practicing, and it will get easier.

It's also important to help others feel good about them. When you say nice things to your friends, it can make them happy. They might start to say nice things to themselves, too. Being kind to others can make you feel good inside. Positive self-talk can help you feel stronger and more confident. It can make hard times easier and good times even better. The more you practice, the better you will get at it. So start today, and keep reminding yourself of all the good things about you.

Creating a Daily Gratitude Practice

Gratitude can help you feel happier and more thankful for the things you have. Gratitude means being thankful and showing appreciation for what you have. Here are some steps to help you start a daily gratitude practice: Every morning, think of one thing you are thankful for. It could be something small, like a sunny day, or something big, like your family. Write it down in a notebook. This is called a gratitude journal. Writing things down helps you remember them and feel more thankful.

When you sit down to eat breakfast, take a moment to think about the food in front of you. Say to yourself. "I am thankful for this food." This can help you appreciate your meal more. Throughout the day, try to notice the good things around you. Maybe you see a pretty flower, hear your favourite song, or a friend makes you laugh. When you notice these things, take a moment to say, "I am thankful for this." This helps you focus on the positive.

At school, think about something you enjoy. It could be a subject you like, a fun project, or playing with friends at recess. During the day, remind yourself, "I am thankful for my school and the things I learn." This can make your school day feel better. When you come home from school, tell your family about one good thing that happened that day. Sharing your gratitude can make you and your family feel happy. You could say, "I am thankful for playing soccer with my friends today," or "I am thankful for learning something new in science."

Before you go to bed, think of three things you are thankful for that happened during the day. Write them down in your gratitude journal. This can help you and your day on a positive note. You might write, "I am thankful for my pet," "I am thankful for my teacher," or "I am thankful for my cozy bed."

You can also show gratitude by doing kind things for others. When you help someone, it can make you both feel good. You could help a friend with homework, hold the door for someone, or say thank you to your bus driver. Doing kind things is a way to show you are thankful for the people around you. Remember to say thank you often.

Surrounding Yourself with Positive People

Yourself important because they can help you feel happy and encouraged. Positive people are those who are kind, supportive, and fun to be around. Here's why it's good to have positive people in your life and how you can find and keep these friends:

Positive people make you feel good about yourself. They say nice things and cheer up when you're feeling down. For example, if you do well on a test, a positive friend might say, "Great job! I knew you could do it!" This can make you feel proud and happy.

When you spend time with positive people, you can have more fun. They often have a good attitude and like to laugh and enjoy life. Playing games, doing hobbies, or just talking with positive friends can make your day better.

Positive people can help you when you have problems. If you are sad or worried, a positive friend will listen to you and try to help. They might give you good advice or just be there to support you. This can make tough times easier to handle. To find positive people, look for friends who are kind and respectful. These are people who treat others nicely and don't say mean things. They include everyone in activities and are not bullies. Being around kind people can make you feel safe and accepted.

Join clubs or groups that interest you. This can be a great way to meet positive people. Whether it's a sports team, art class, or science club, you can find friends who like the same things you do. Shared interests can help you bond and build strong friendships. Be a positive person yourself. Smile, say nice things, and help others. When you are kind and friendly, you attract positive people. They will want to be around you because you make them feel good, too.

If someone is being negative, try not to let it affect you. Negative people might say unkind things or make you feel bad about yourself. It's okay to spend less time with people who bring you down. Focus on those who lift you up and make you happy.

Encourage your friends and family to be positive. Sometimes, people don't realize they are being negative. If a friend is upset, try to cheer them up. You could say, "I'm here for you," or "Let's think of something fun to do." Helping others feel better can create a positive atmosphere.

Remember to be patient with yourself and others. Everyone has bad days, and sometimes even positive people can feel sad or upset. It's important to be understanding and supportive. If a friend is having a hard time, just being there and listening can help a lot.

Practice gratitude with your friends. Share things you are thankful for and encourage your friends to do the same. This can help everyone focus on the good things in life and feel more positive. Spend time with family members who make you feel good. Family can be a great source of positivity. Talk to your parents, siblings, or grandparents about your day. Share your thoughts and listen to theirs. Family members can give you love and support that makes you feel happy.

Surrounding yourself with positive people can make your life brighter and more joyful. Positive friends help you feel good about yourself, have fun, and get through tough times. By being kind and seeking out positive relationships, you can create a happy and supportive circle of friends and family. Remember, you deserve to be around people who make you feel good!

Visualizing Success

Success is a powerful way to help you achieve your goals and feel more confident. Visualizing means creating a picture in your mind of what you want to happen. When you imagine yourself being successful, it can help you feel more positive and motivated. Here's how you can practice visualizing success: First, think about what you want to achieve. It could be doing well on a test, winning a game, or learning a new skill. Pick a goal that is important to you. For example, if you want to do well on a math test, make that your goal.

Find a quiet place where you can sit comfortably. Close your eyes and take a few deep breaths to relax. This can help you focus better on your visualization. Now, imagine yourself achieving your goal. Picture it in your mind as clearly as you can. If your goal is to do well on a test, imagine yourself sitting at your desk, answering the questions confidently, and getting a good grade.

Think about the details. What do you see around you? What sounds do you hear? How do you feel? The more details you imagine, the more real it will feel. If you are visualizing winning a game, imagine the crowd cheering, your teammates celebrating, and the feeling of happiness. See yourself succeeding step by step. If your goal is to learn a new skill, imagine yourself practicing and getting better each day. Visualize yourself finally mastering the skill and feeling proud of your accomplishment.

Use positive self-talk while you visualize. Say things to yourself like, "I can do this," "I am prepared," and "I will succeed." These positive statements can boost your confidence and make your visualization stronger. Practice visualizing success regularly. You can do it every morning when you wake up or every night before you go to bed. The more you practice, the easier it will become and the more effective it will be. Visualize not only the success but also the hard work and effort you put in to get there. Imagine yourself studying hard for the test, practicing for the game, or working on your new skill. This helps you understand that success comes from hard work and persistence.

If you face challenges, visualize yourself overcoming them. Imagine finding solutions and staying strong even when things get tough. This can help you feel more prepared and resilient in real life. You can also create a vision board. A vision board is a collection of pictures and words that represent your goals and dreams. You can cut out pictures from magazines or draw your own. Look at your vision board every day to remind yourself of your goals and keep your motivation high.

Share your goals and visualizations with a trusted friend or family member. Talking about your dreams can make them feel more real and give you extra support and encouragement. Remember, visualizing success is just one part of achieving your goals. You also need to take action and work hard. Visualization can give you the confidence and motivation to do your best, but you still need to put in the effort.

Finally, believe in yourself. Trust that you have the ability to achieve your goals. When you visualize success and work hard, you can accomplish amazing things. Visualizing success can help you feel more confident and motivated. By imagining yourself achieving your goals, you can create a positive mindset and boost your chances of success. Practice regularly, stay positive, and remember to put in the hard work. You can achieve great things!

Letting Go of Negative Self-Comparisons

Important for feeling happy and confident. Negative self-comparisons happen when you compare yourself to others and feel bad because you think they are better. Here are some ways to stop comparing yourself negatively and start feeling better about whom you are; First, remember that everyone is different. Everyone has their own strengths and weaknesses. Just because someone is good at something doesn't mean you have to be good at it too. Celebrate what makes you unique. For example, you might be great at drawing while your friend is good at playing soccer. Both are special talents.

Focus on your own progress, not someone else's. Think about how much you've improved in different areas of your life. Maybe you're getting better at math, reading more books, or learning to play an instrument. These are things to be proud of. Your journey is your own, and it's important to see how far you've come.

Practice gratitude for what you have. Make a list of things you like about yourself and things you're thankful for. This can help you see the positive things in your life and feel happier. For example, you might be thankful for your family, your friends, your home, or your hobbies. Gratitude helps you focus on the good things rather than comparing yourself to others.

When you notice yourself comparing to others, try to change your thoughts. Instead of thinking, "They are so much better than me," think, "I am doing my best, and that's enough." Positive self-talk can help you feel more confident and less worried about others. Remember, everyone has their own pace and it's okay to be different.

Spend time doing things you enjoy. When you are busy with activities you like, you have less time to compare yourself to others. Play sports, draw, read, or spend time with friends. Doing what makes you happy can help you feel good about yourself. Enjoying your hobbies and interests can boost your self-esteem.

Remember that what you see isn't always the whole story. People often share only the best parts of their lives, especially on social media. They don't show the hard times or struggles they go through. Keep this in mind when you see pictures or stories that make you feel like you're not as good as others. Everyone has challenges, even if they don't show them.

Set your own goals based on what you want, not what others are doing? Think about what makes you happy and what you want to achieve. Your goals should be about improving yourself, not competing with others. If you love painting, set a goal to finish a new painting each month, regardless of what others are doing. Talk to someone you trust about how you feel. Sharing your thoughts and feelings with a parent, teacher, or friend can help you feel better. They can offer support and remind you of your strengths. Sometimes just talking about your worries can make them seem smaller.

Celebrate your achievements, no matter how small. Every step you take towards your goals is important. Whether it's finishing a book, getting a good grade, or learning a new song on an instrument, gives yourself credit for your hard work. This helps you focus on your own successes instead of comparing them to others.

Remember, everyone has their own path and their own struggles. Just because someone else seems to have it all doesn't mean they do. Focus on being the best version of yourself. Be proud of who you are and what you can do. You are unique and valuable just as you are.

Letting go of negative self-comparisons can help you feel happier and more confident. By focusing on your own strengths, practicing gratitude, and setting personal goals, you can build a positive self-image. Remember to be kind to yourself and celebrate your own achievements.

Chapter Summary

1. Positive self-talk can help you feel stronger and more confident.

2. Gratitude encourage us to appreciate every good things that comes our way and express continuous thanks.

3. Positive people make you feel good about yourself.

4. Visualization is powerful achieving your goal. Imagine what you like, keep. practice every day it will parts of your life.

5. Focus on being the best version of yourself. Be proud of who you are and what you can do.

6. TAKING ACTION EVERY DAY

"Success seems to be connected with action.
Successful people keep moving.
They make mistakes but they don't quit"

– Conrad Hilton

Creating a Daily Action Plan

Creating a daily action plan can help you stay organized and get things done. A daily action plan is a list of tasks you want to complete each day. It helps you know what to do and when to do it. Here's how you can make a daily action plan first, get a notebook or a piece of paper. You can also use a planner if you have one. Write the date at the top so you know which day the plan is for.

Next, think about what you need to do that day. Make a list of tasks. These can be school assignments, chores, or activities. For example, your list might include doing homework, cleaning your room, practicing an instrument, and playing outside. Prioritize your tasks. Put the most important tasks at the top of your list. This helps you know what to focus on first. For example, if you have a test tomorrow, studying for it should be at the top of your list.

Break big tasks into smaller steps. If you have a big project, divide it into smaller, manageable parts. This makes it easier to complete. For example, if you have a science project, your steps might be, research, write notes, create a poster, and practice your presentation.

Set a time for each task. Decide when you will do each task during the day. You can write the time next to each task on your list. For example, you might write: "3:00 PM – Math homework" and "4:00 PM – Practice piano." This helps you manage your time well. Include breaks in your plan. It's important to take short breaks to rest and recharge. After working on a task for a while, take a 10-15 minute break. You can write these breaks into your plan. For example, after finishing your math homework, take a break to have a snack or go for a short walk.

Check off tasks as you complete them. When you finish a task, put a check mark next to it on your list. This helps you see your progress and feel accomplished. It's a good feeling to see how much you've done!

Be flexible with your plan. Sometimes things don't go as expected, and that's okay. If something takes longer than planned or you need to move a task to another time, adjust your plan. The goal is to stay organized, not to be perfect.

Review your plan at the end of the day. Look at what you accomplished and think about what you can do better tomorrow. Celebrate the tasks you completed and make a note of any tasks you need to move to the next day.

Use your daily action plan every day. Making a plan each day helps you build good habits and stay on track. It can make your days smoother and less stressful. Remember to include time for fun activities. Your action plan isn't just for work, it's also for play. Make sure you have time for hobbies, playing with friends, and relaxing. Balance is important.

Talk to a parent or teacher if you need help with your plan. They can give you advice on how to organize your tasks and manage your time. It's okay to ask for help. Creating a daily action plan helps you stay organized and get things done. By writing down your tasks, prioritizing them, and setting a time for each one, you can make your day more productive and enjoyable. Don't forget to include breaks and fun activities to keep things balanced. Practice making a plan every day, and you'll find it gets easier and more helpful. You can do it!

Setting Aside Time for Goal-Related Activities

You achieve what you want to do. Goals are things you want to accomplish, like learning to play a new song on the piano, reading a book, or getting better at a sport. Here's how you can make time for your goals: First, decide what your goal is. Think about what you want to achieve. For example, maybe your goal is to improve your basketball skills or finish reading a book. Write down your goal to help you remember it.

Next, make a plan. Think about what steps you need to take to reach your goal. If your goal is to get better at basketball, your steps might include practicing dribbling, shooting, and playing games. If your goal is to finish reading a book, your steps might include reading a chapter each day.

Look at your daily schedule. See where you have free time. You might have free time after school, before dinner, or on weekends. Find a time that works best for you to focus on your goal.

Set aside a specific time each day for your goal-related activities. This means choosing a time when you will work on your goal every day. For example, you might decide to practice basketball from 4:00 PM to 4:30 PM every day. Write this time in your planner or make a note of it. Stick to your schedule. Try to do your goal-related activity at the same time every day. This helps you build a routine and make it a habit. If you practice regularly, you will get better and closer to achieving your goal.

Start with small steps. If you try to do too much at once, you might feel overwhelmed. Begin with a small, manageable amount of time, like 15 or 20 minutes. As you get used to your routine, you can increase the time you spend on your goal.

Be consistent. It's important to work on your goal every day, even if it's just for a little while. Consistency helps you make steady progress. Remember, it's okay if you don't see results right away. Keep practicing, and you will improve over time.

Stay focused during your goal-related time. Try to avoid distractions like TV or video games. Find a quiet place where you can concentrate. This will help you make the most of the time you set aside.

Ask for help if you need it. If you're having trouble with your goal, talk to a parent, teacher, or coach. They can give you tips and support to help you succeed.

Celebrate your progress. Every time you reach a milestone or complete a step towards your goal, take a moment to feel proud of yourself. For example, if you learned a new basketball move or finished a chapter of your book, celebrate your achievement. This can motivate you to keep going.

Adjust your plan if needed. Sometimes things don't go as planned, and that's okay. If you need more time for a step or if something isn't working, change your plan. The important thing is to keep moving forward.

Be patient with yourself. Reaching a goal can take time, and it's normal to face challenges along the way. Don't get discouraged if things are tough. Keep trying, and remember that every bit of effort brings you closer to your goal.

Balance your time. Make sure you also have time for other activities, like homework, chores, and fun with friends. It's important to have a balanced schedule so you don't get too tired or stressed.

Setting aside time for goal-related activities helps you stay focused and make progress. By planning your time, staying consistent, and celebrating your successes, you can achieve your goals. Remember to be patient and enjoy the journey. You can accomplish great things with dedication and effort!

Breaking Tasks into Manageable Steps

Like turning a big job into smaller, easier pieces. It's a way to make things less scary and more doable. Imagine you have to clean your messy room. Instead of feeling overwhelmed by the whole mess, you can break it down into smaller steps to make it easier to handle.

First, start by looking around your room and deciding what needs to be done. You might see clothes on the floor, toys scattered everywhere, and books piled up on your desk. Write down each thing you need to do, like picking up the clothes, putting away the toys, and organizing the books.

Once you have your list, think about what order to do things in. It might make sense to start with the clothes since they're on the floor and could be tripped over. Then you could move on to the toys and finally the books. By putting your tasks in order, you can tackle them one by one without feeling overwhelmed.

Now that you have your plan, it's time to get started. Begin with the first step on your list, which is picking up the clothes. Take each piece of clothing and put it where it belongs – in the closet or the laundry basket. As you finish each item, check it off your list. It feels good to see your progress! After the clothes are picked up, move on to the next step – putting away the toys. Start by gathering them all up and then find a place for each toy to go. You might have bins or shelves where toys can be stored. Put each toy in its place and check it off your list when you're done.

Finally, it's time to tackle the books. Sort through them and decide where each one should go. You might want to organize them by size, color, or type of book. Once they're all in order, your room will look neat and tidy.

Throughout the process, take breaks if you need them. Cleaning can be hard work, and it's okay to rest for a bit before moving on to the next step. You could take a snack break, play with a toy for a few minutes, or read a book.

If you get stuck or feel overwhelmed, don't be afraid to ask for help. Your parents or siblings might be willing to lend a hand and make the task go faster. Working together can also make cleaning more fun! As you complete each step, take a moment to appreciate your progress. You started with a messy room, and now it's clean and organized – all because you broke the task into manageable steps and tackled them one by one.

Breaking tasks into manageable steps can make even the biggest jobs feel easier. Whether it's cleaning your room, doing homework, or practicing a new skill, taking things one step at a time helps you stay focused and motivated. With a little planning and effort, you can accomplish anything!

Tracking Your Progress

Tracking your progress means keeping an eye on how well you're doing as you work towards a goal. It's like drawing a map to see how far you've come and how much further you have to go. Here's how you can track your progress: First, decide on a goal you want to achieve. It could be something like getting better at math, learning a new song on the piano, or reading a certain number of books. Write down your goal so you remember what you're working towards.

Next, break your goal into smaller steps. This makes it easier to see your progress along the way. For example, if your goal is to get better at math, your steps might include practicing addition, subtraction, multiplication, and division. Each time you complete a step, you're one step closer to your goal.

Once you have your steps, decide how you'll track your progress. You could use a chart, a graph, or a checklist. For example, if your goal is to read 10 books, you could make a chart with 10 boxes and color in one box each time you finish a book. This helps you see how many books you've read and how many you have left to read.

Start working towards your goal and keep track of your progress as you go. Each time you complete a step, mark it off on your chart or checklist. This helps you stay motivated and focused on your goal.

Celebrate your successes along the way. When you reach a milestone or complete a step, take a moment to pat yourself on the back. You're making progress, and that's something to be proud of! If you notice you're falling behind or having trouble with a step, don't get discouraged. Instead, think about what you can do to get back on track. Maybe you need to spend more time practicing, ask for help from a teacher or parent, or break the step down into smaller parts.

Keep track of any obstacles or challenges you encounter. This can help you learn from your experiences and find ways to overcome similar obstacles in the future. For example, if you're having trouble with a math problem, write down what you're struggling with and how you plan to solve it. This can help you remember what you've learned and make it easier to tackle similar problems later on.

Review your progress regularly. Take a look at your chart or checklist and see how far you've come. This can help you stay motivated and remind you of why you set the goal in the first place. If you're close to reaching your goal, keep pushing yourself to finish strong. If you still have a long way to go, break the remaining steps down into smaller parts and keep working towards your goal.

Remember that progress doesn't always happen in a straight line. There will be ups and downs along the way, but as long as you keep working towards your goal, you'll get there eventually. Keep track of your progress, stay focused, and don't give up. You can do it.

Celebrating Small Wins Along the Way

Celebrating small wins along the way means taking time to recognize and feel proud of the little achievements you make as you work towards a bigger goal. It's like giving yourself a high-five or a pat on the back for each step you take in the right direction. Here's why celebrating small wins is important and how you can do it:

First, let's talk about why celebrating small wins is a big deal. When you set a big goal for yourself, like learning to ride a bike or getting better at math, it can sometimes feel like you'll never get there. But when you break that big goal into smaller steps and celebrate each one you complete, it helps you see that you're making progress. It's like climbing a mountain – each step you take gets you a little closer to the top, and celebrating each step gives you the energy and motivation to keep going.

So how can you celebrate small wins? There are lots of ways to do it, and it's all about finding what works best for you. Here are some ideas:

⮝ Give yourself a pat on the back. When you finish a step towards your goal, take a moment to acknowledge your hard work and feel proud of yourself. You could literally pat yourself on the back or just say to yourself, "Good job, me!"

⮝ Do a happy dance. Put on your favourite song and dance around to celebrate your achievement. It's a fun way to let off some steam and boost your mood.

⮝ Treat yourself to something special. It doesn't have to be anything big – maybe just a small snack or some extra playtime. The important thing is to take a moment to reward yourself for your hard work.

⮝ Share your success with someone else. Tell a friend, family member, or teacher about what you've accomplished. They can cheer you on and celebrate with you, which can make your win even sweeter.

⮝ Keep track of your wins. Make a chart or a checklist and mark off each step you complete towards your goal. Seeing all the progress you've made can be really motivating and remind you of how far you've come.

Remember, celebrating small wins isn't just about feeling good in the moment – it's also about building confidence and momentum to keep moving forward. So don't be afraid to take a moment to pat you on the back and say, "Great job!" You're doing amazing things, and you deserve to celebrate every step of the way!

Chapter Summary

1. A daily action plan is list of tasks you want to complete each day.

2. It's important to work on your goal. every day write this time I practice for this work.(Ex) 4 pm to 4.30 pm practice for basketball.

3. Breaking tasks into manageable steps can make even the biggest jobs feel easier. (Ex) Pomodoro Technique..

4. Review your progress regularly. Stay focused and don't give up. you can do it,

5. Celebrating small wins when achieve task. Give yourself a pat on the back

7. BUILDING CONFIDENCE AND BELIEF

"Believe you can and you're half way there"

–Theodore Roosevelt

Reflecting on Past Achievements

Thinking back on the things you've accomplished in the past and remembering how they made you feel. It's like looking in a mirror and seeing all the cool things you've done staring back at you. Here's why reflecting on past achievements is important and how you can do it: First, let's talk about why reflecting on past achievements is a big deal. When you think back on things you've accomplished in the past, it helps you see how much you've grown and changed over time. It's like looking at a photo album of your life and seeing all the cool stuff you've done. Remembering your past achievements can also give you a confidence boost and remind you that you're capable of doing great things.

So how can you reflect on past achievements? It's easy — just take a trip down memory lane and think about all the cool stuff you've done in the past. Here are some ideas to get you started:

▲ Make a list of your achievements. Sit down with a piece of paper and write down all the things you've accomplished in your life so far. It could be anything — like learning to ride a bike, getting a good grade on a test, or winning an award. Seeing your achievements written down can help you appreciate how awesome you are!

▲ Look through old photos or keepsakes. Dig out your old photo albums, scrapbooks, or memory boxes and take a trip down memory lane. Look at all the cool stuff you've done in the past and remember how it made you feel. You might even find some forgotten treasures hiding in there!

▲ Talk to someone about your achievements. Share your accomplishments with a friend, family member, or teacher. They can help you celebrate your successes and remind you of how awesome you are. Plus, it's always fun to share good news with someone else!

▲ Think about how your achievements have shaped you. Reflect on how your past achievements have helped you grow and learn. Maybe you've become more confident, resilient, or determined as a result of your accomplishments. Remembering how far you've come can help you feel proud of yourself and excited for the future.

⅄ Use your past achievements to set new goals. Think about the things you've accomplished in the past and use them as inspiration for new goals. Maybe you want to learn a new skill, achieve a higher grade in school, or try something new. Reflecting on your past achievements can give you the confidence and motivation to tackle new challenges head-on.

Remember, reflecting on past achievements isn't about bragging or showing off – it's about appreciating how far you've come and feeling proud of yourself. So take a moment to think back on all the cool stuff you've done in the past, and give you a big pat on the back. You're awesome, and you deserve to celebrate all the amazing things you've accomplished.

Challenging Negative Self-doubt

Self - Doubt means not letting those mean thoughts in your head convince you that you can't do something. It's like telling a bully to go away and not bother you anymore. Here's why challenging negative self-doubt is important and how you can do it:

First, let's talk about why negative self-doubt can be a big problem. Sometimes, when you're trying to do something new or difficult, those sneaky thoughts in your head might try to convince you that you're not good enough or that you'll fail. It's like having a little voice inside your head saying mean things about you. But here's the thing – those thoughts are just that, thoughts. They're not facts, and they don't have to control how you feel or what you do.

So how can you challenge negative self-doubt? It's all about learning to recognize those mean thoughts for what they are – just thoughts – and not letting them stop you from doing what you want to do. Here are some tips to help you challenge negative self-doubt:

- **Pay attention to your thoughts**. When you start to feel doubt creeping in, take a moment to notice what you're thinking. Are you telling yourself things like "I'm not good enough" or "I'll never be able to do this"? Recognizing these negative thoughts is the first step to challenging them.

- **Question your thoughts**. Once you've noticed your negative thoughts, ask yourself if they're really true. Are you really not good enough, or are you just feeling nervous because you're trying something new? Chances are, those negative thoughts are just exaggerating the situation and making you feel worse than you need to.

- **Replace negative thoughts with positive ones.** Instead of telling yourself "I can't do this," try saying something like "I can do hard things" or "I'll give it my best shot." Positive affirmations like these can help boost your confidence and remind you that you're capable of overcoming challenges.

- ⬥ **Focus on your strengths.** When negative self-doubt starts to creep in, take a moment to think about all the things you're good at. Maybe you're a great artist, a fast runner, or a good friend. Remembering your strengths can help you feel more confident and remind you that you're capable of doing amazing things.

- ⬥ **Take action despite your doubts.** Sometimes, the best way to challenge negative self-doubt is to prove it wrong. Instead of letting those mean thoughts stop you from trying, take a deep breath and dive in. You might surprise yourself with what you can accomplish when you push past your doubts and give it your best shot.

Remember, challenging negative self-doubt takes practice, and it's okay if you don't get it right every time. The important thing is to keep trying and not let those mean thoughts hold you back. You're capable of amazing things, and you deserve to believe in yourself.

Stepping Out of Your Comfort Zone

Stepping comfort zone means trying new things or doing things that might feel a little scary at first. It's like venturing into uncharted territory or exploring a new world. Here's why stepping out of your comfort zone is important and how you can do it:

First, let's talk about why stepping out of your comfort zone is a big deal. Your comfort zone is like a cozy bubble where everything feels safe and familiar. It's where you feel comfortable and confident because you know what to expect. But here's the thing – growth and learning happen outside of your comfort zone. When you try new things or take on new challenges, you stretch yourself and discover what you're capable of. Stepping out of your comfort zone can help you build confidence, resilience, and new skills.

So how can you step out of your comfort zone? It's all about taking small steps and being willing to try new things, even if they feel a little scary at first. Here are some tips to help you step out of your comfort zone:

- **Start small.** You don't have to jump into the deep end right away – just dip your toe in the water and see how it feels. Try something new that's just a little outside of your comfort zone, like talking to someone new at school or trying a new food. As you get more comfortable, you can gradually push yourself to try bigger challenges.

- **Take risks.** Stepping out of your comfort zone means taking risks and trying things that might not work out perfectly. But that's okay – making mistakes is how we learn and grow. Embrace the idea of trying and failing, and don't be afraid to take risks along the way.

⋏ **Challenge yourself.** Set goals that push you out of your comfort zone and give you something to work towards. Maybe you want to try out for a sports team, give a presentation in class, or learn to play a musical instrument. Whatever it is, challenge yourself to step outside of what feels safe and comfortable.

⋏ **Be open-minded.** Stepping out of your comfort zone means being open to new experiences and perspectives. Keep an open mind and be willing to try things that might be different from what you're used to. You never know – you might discover something new that you love!

⋏ **Celebrate your successes.** When you step out of your comfort zone and try something new, take a moment to pat yourself on the back and celebrate your courage. Even if things don't go perfectly, give yourself credit for having the courage to try. Every step you take outside of your comfort zone is a step towards growth and learning.

Remember, stepping out of your comfort zone can feel scary at first, but it's also incredibly rewarding. When you push yourself to try new things and take on new challenges, you're expanding your horizons and discovering what you're truly capable of. So don't be afraid to take that first step outside of your comfort zone – you never know what amazing adventures await you.

Practicing Self-Compassion

Being kind to yourself, just like you would be to a good friend. It's like giving yourself a warm hug or a pat on the back when you're feeling down. Here's why practicing self-compassion is important and how you can do it:

First, let's talk about why practicing self-compassion is a big deal. Sometimes, when things don't go the way we want them to or when we make a mistake, we can be really hard on ourselves. We might say mean things to ourselves like "I'm so stupid" or "I'll never get it right." But here's the thing – being hard on yourself doesn't help anything. In fact, it can make you feel even worse. That's where self-compassion comes in. Instead of beating yourself up when things go wrong, self-compassion means treating yourself with kindness and understanding.

So how can you practice self-compassion? It's all about being gentle with yourself and treating yourself with the same care and kindness you would show to a good friend. Here are some tips to help you practice self-compassion:

- **Be mindful of your thoughts.** Pay attention to the things you say to yourself when things don't go the way you want them to. Are you being kind and supportive, or are you being critical and harsh? Notice when you're being hard on yourself and try to replace those negative thoughts with kinder ones.

⋏ **Treat yourself with kindness.** When you're feeling down or disappointed, imagine what you would say to a good friend who was going through the same thing. Would you tell them they're stupid or worthless? Of course not! You would probably say something like "It's okay, everyone makes mistakes" or "You're doing the best you can." Treat yourself with the same kindness and understanding.

⋏ **Practice self-care.** Taking care of yourself is an important part of self-compassion. Make time for activities that make you feel good, like reading a book, going for a walk, or spending time with friends. Taking care of yourself helps you feel happier and more resilient, which makes it easier to be kind to yourself.

⋏ **Forgive yourself.** We all make mistakes – it's a part of being human. Instead of dwelling on your mistakes or beating yourself up for them, try to forgive yourself and move on. Remember that everyone messes up sometimes, and it doesn't make you any less lovable or worthy.

⋏ **Be your own cheerleader.** Instead of waiting for someone else to praise you or give you permission to feel good about yourself, be your own biggest fan. Celebrate your successes, no matter how small, and give yourself credit for the things you do well. You deserve to feel proud of yourself!

Remember, practicing self-compassion is like giving yourself a gift – the gift of kindness and understanding. By treating yourself with the same care and compassion you would show to a good friend, you can build resilience, boost your self-esteem, and feel happier and more confident in yourself. So be gentle with yourself, be kind to yourself, and remember that you're worthy of love and compassion just as you are.

Building a Supportive Network of Friends and Family

Surrounding yourself with people who care about you, cheer you on, and help you when you need it. It's like having a team of superheroes who always have your back and make you feel safe and loved. Here's why building a supportive network is important and how you can do it:

First, let's talk about why having a supportive network is a big deal. Life can be full of ups and downs, and it's normal to feel happy, sad, excited, or scared sometimes. But when you have people you can turn to for support, it makes those ups and downs a little easier to handle. Whether you need a shoulder to cry on, someone to celebrate with, or just a listening ear, having supportive friends and family can make all the difference.

So how can you build a supportive network of friends and family? It's all about reaching out, being kind, and being there for others in return. Here are some tips to help you build a supportive network:

⅄ **Be a good friend.** Treat others the way you want to be treated. Be kind, supportive, and respectful to your friends and classmates. Listen when they need to talk, offer a helping hand when they need it, and celebrate their successes with them.

⅄ **Reach out to others.** Don't be afraid to make the first move and reach out to new people. Smile, say hello, and start a conversation. You never know – you might just make a new friend!

⅄ **Share your feelings.** Opening up to others about how you're feeling can help strengthen your relationships and build trust. If you're feeling sad, scared, or worried, don't be afraid to talk to someone you trust about it. Chances are, they've been there too and can offer support and understanding.

⅄ **Be there for others.** When someone you care about is going through a tough time, be there for them. Offer a listening ear, a comforting hug, or a word of encouragement. Let them know that you're there for them no matter what.

⅄ **Spend time together.** Building strong relationships takes time and effort, so make sure to spend quality time with your friends and family. Whether you're playing games, going for a walk, or just hanging out and talking, spending time together helps strengthen your bonds and build trust.

➤ **Be patient.** Building a supportive network of friends and family doesn't happen overnight. It takes time to develop meaningful relationships and build trust. Be patient with yourself and others, and keep putting in the effort to nurture your connections.

Remember, having a supportive network of friends and family can make life's challenges a little easier to bear and life's joys a little sweeter to celebrate. So reach out, be kind, and be there for each other – you never know when you might need a superhero to save the day.

Chapter Summary

1. Reflect on how your past achievements have helped you grow and Learn.

2. Focus on your strengths. It help you feel more confident. Material of doing anything.

3. Every step you take outside comfort zone is a step towards growth and Learning.

4. Taking care of yourself is an important part of self-compassion.

5. Having supportive net work of friends and family can make life's challenges a Little easier.

8. EMBRACING FAILURE AS A STEPPING STONE

❖

"Failure is simply the opportunity to begin again, this time more intelligently"

– Henry Ford

Reframing Failure as a Learning Opportunity

Looking at mistakes or setbacks as chances to grow and improve, rather than as reasons to feel bad about you. It's like turning lemons into lemonade or finding a silver lining in a cloudy sky. Here's why reframing failure is important and how you can do it:

First, let's talk about why reframing failure is a big deal. Nobody likes to fail – it can feel embarrassing, disappointing, or even scary. But here's the thing – failure is a natural part of life, and everyone experiences it at one time or another. The key is not to let failure hold you back or make you feel bad about yourself. Instead, think of failure as a valuable learning experience that can help you grow and improve.

So how can you reframe failure as a learning opportunity? It's all about changing the way you think about failure and finding the lessons in your mistakes. Here are some tips to help you reframe failure:

- ▲ **Change your perspective.** Instead of seeing failure as a sign that you're not good enough or that you'll never succeed, try to see it as a normal part of the learning process. Everyone makes mistakes, and failing at something doesn't mean you're a failure – it just means you haven't figured it out yet.

- ▲ **Focus on what you can learn.** When you experience failure, take a step back and think about what went wrong and what you can learn from the experience. Maybe you discovered a new way not to do something, or you realized that you need to practice more or ask for help. Finding the lessons in your mistakes can help you grow and improve.

- ▲ **Celebrate your efforts.** Even if you didn't achieve the outcome you were hoping for, give yourself credit for trying. Putting yourself out there and taking risks is brave, and it's something to be proud of, regardless of the outcome. Celebrate your efforts and remind yourself that failure is just a temporary setback on the road to success.

- **Keep trying.** Don't let failure stop you from pursuing your goals and dreams. Instead, use it as motivation to keep going and keep trying. Remember that every successful person has experienced failure along the way – it's how they respond to failure that sets them apart.

- **Practice self-compassion.** Be kind to yourself when you experience failure. Instead of beating yourself up or feeling bad about yourself, practice self-compassion and treat yourself with kindness and understanding. Remember that failure is a normal part of life, and it doesn't define your worth as a person.

Remember, reframing failure as a learning opportunity takes practice, but it's a valuable skill that can help you grow and succeed in life. So the next time you experience failure, take a deep breath, reframe your thinking, and remember that every setback is just a chance to learn and grow.

Understanding That Failure is a Normal Part of Growth

Knowing that making mistakes or not succeeding at something doesn't mean you're not good enough. It's like realizing that falling off your bike when you're learning to ride doesn't mean you'll never be able to ride it. Here's why understanding this is important and how you can do it:

First, let's talk about why knowing that failure is normal is a big deal. Sometimes, when we try something new or challenging, we might make mistakes or not do as well as we hoped. And that's okay – it doesn't mean we're not smart or talented. In fact, it's often through making mistakes and learning from them that we grow and improve. Understanding that failure is a normal part of growth can help us feel less afraid to try new things and more confident in ourselves.

So how can you understand that failure is a normal part of growth? It's all about changing the way you think about failure and recognizing its role in the learning process. Here are some tips to help you understand this concept:

- **Know that everyone makes mistakes.** Nobody is perfect – not even adults! We all make mistakes from time to time, and that's okay. Making mistakes is how we learn and grow. So if you mess up or don't do as well as you hoped, remember that you're not alone – everyone has been there.

- **See failure as a learning opportunity.** Instead of seeing failure as something to be ashamed of or afraid of, try to see it as a chance to learn and improve. When you make a mistake, ask yourself what you can learn from it. Maybe you'll realize that you need to practice more, ask for help, or try a different approach next time. Finding the lessons in your mistakes can help you grow and become better at whatever you're trying to do.

- ⋏ **Remember that failure is temporary.** Just because you fail at something doesn't mean you'll fail forever. Failure is just a temporary setback on the road to success. So if you don't succeed at something right away, don't give up. Keep trying, keep learning, and keep growing. You'll get there eventually!

- ⋏ **Celebrate your efforts, not just your successes.** Success isn't just about achieving a certain outcome – it's also about the effort you put in along the way. So even if you don't succeed at something, give yourself credit for trying. Celebrate your efforts and remind yourself that you're brave and capable for trying something new or challenging.

- ⋏ **Practice self-compassion.** Be kind to yourself when you experience failure. Instead of being hard on yourself or feeling bad about yourself, practice self-compassion and treat yourself with kindness and understanding. Remember that everyone fails sometimes, and it doesn't mean you're not good enough or worthy of love and respect.

Understanding that failure is a normal part of growth can help you feel more confident, resilient, and willing to take risks in life. So the next time you make a mistake or don't succeed at something, remember that it's just a bump in the road – not the end of the journey. Keep learning, keep growing, and keep believing in yourself.

Seeking Feedback After Setbacks

Asking for advice or suggestions from others when things don't go the way you hoped. It's like asking a friend for help figuring out a puzzle when you can't find the right piece. Here's why seeking feedback is important and how you can do it: First, let's talk about why seeking feedback after setbacks is a big deal. When something doesn't go the way you planned or you make a mistake, it can be frustrating and confusing. But instead of getting upset or giving up, seeking feedback can help you figure out what went wrong and how you can do better next time. It's like having a map to help you find your way when you're feeling lost.

So how can you seek feedback after setbacks? It's all about being open to learning from your experiences and asking for help when you need it. Here are some tips to help you seek feedback:

- ⅄ **Ask for feedback from someone you trust.** This could be a teacher, a parent, a coach, or a friend – someone who knows you well and wants to see you succeed. Tell them what happened and ask for their honest opinion about what went wrong and how you can improve.

- ⅄ **Listen carefully to the feedback you receive.** When someone gives you feedback, listen with an open mind and really try to understand what they're saying. Even if it's not what you wanted to hear, remember that feedback is meant to help you grow and improve.

- **Ask questions if you don't understand.** If you're not sure what someone means or you need more information, don't be afraid to ask questions. It's better to ask for clarification than to guess and misunderstand.

- **Use the feedback to make a plan.** Once you've received feedback, think about how you can use it to improve. Maybe you need to practice more, ask for help from a teacher or coach, or try a different approach next time. Make a plan and set goals for yourself based on the feedback you received.

- **Don't take feedback personally.** Remember that feedback is about your actions or behaviour, not about you as a person. So even if someone tells you that you made a mistake or could have done better, try not to take it personally. Instead, use the feedback as an opportunity to learn and grow.

- **Thank the person for their feedback.** It's important to show appreciation for the time and effort someone puts into giving you feedback. So be sure to thank them for their help, even if the feedback wasn't exactly what you wanted to hear.

Remember, seeking feedback after setbacks is a sign of strength, not weakness. It shows that you're willing to learn from your experiences and take responsibility for your actions. So don't be afraid to ask for help when you need it – it's the first step towards growing and improving as a person.

Viewing Failure as a Temporary Setback

Understanding that when things don't go as planned or when you make mistakes, it doesn't mean you can't succeed in the future. It's like thinking of a speed bump on the road – it slows you down for a bit, but you can keep moving forward afterward. Here's why seeing failure this way is important and how you can do it:

First, let's talk about why seeing failure as a temporary setback is a big deal. When you try something new or work toward a goal, it's normal to face challenges and setbacks along the way. These setbacks might make you feel disappointed or frustrated, but it's important to remember that they're not the end of the road. Seeing failure as a temporary setback can help you stay positive and motivated to keep trying, even when things get tough.

So how can you view failure as a temporary setback? It's all about changing the way you think about failure and understanding that it's just a bump in the road, not the end of your journey. Here are some tips to help you do that:

- **Remember that everyone fails sometimes.** Nobody is perfect, and everyone experiences failure at one time or another. Even the most successful people in the world have faced setbacks and challenges on their journey to success. Knowing that you're not alone can help you feel better about your own failures and setbacks.

▲ **Think of failure as a learning experience.** Instead of dwelling on your mistakes or feeling discouraged, try to see failure as an opportunity to learn and grow. Ask yourself what you can learn from the experience and how you can use it to do better next time. Maybe you discovered a new approach that didn't work, or maybe you realized that you need to practice more. Finding the lessons in your failures can help you become stronger and more resilient.

▲ **Keep things in perspective.** When you experience failure, try not to blow it out of proportion or let it define you. Remember that failure is just a temporary setback, not a reflection of your worth as a person. Keep things in perspective and remind yourself that you're capable of overcoming challenges and achieving your goals.

▲ **Stay positive and resilient.** Instead of dwelling on your failures or giving up when things get tough, try to stay positive and resilient. Focus on the things you can control, like your attitude and effort, and keep moving forward one step at a time. Remember that setbacks are just a natural part of the journey to success, and they can make you stronger and more determined in the long run.

▲ **Celebrate your progress.** Even if you haven't reached your ultimate goal yet, take time to celebrate the progress you've made along the way. Whether it's a small step forward or a big milestone, every bit of progress is worth celebrating. Recognizing your achievements can help you stay motivated and focused on your goals.

Remember, failure is not the end of the road – it's just a temporary setback on the journey to success. By changing the way you think about failure and seeing it as an opportunity to learn and grow, you can stay positive and motivated even when things get tough. So keep moving forward, keep learning from your mistakes, and keep believing in yourself.

Using Failure as Motivation to Keep Going

Turning setbacks or mistakes into fuel for your determination and perseverance. It's like using a bump in the road to push you forward instead of holding you back. Here's why using failure as motivation is important and how you can do it:

First, let's talk about why using failure as motivation is a big deal. When you experience failure, it can feel discouraging and make you want to give up. But instead of letting failure defeat you, using it as motivation can help you stay focused on your goals and keep moving forward. It's like turning lemons into lemonade – finding something positive in a negative situation.

So how can you use failure as motivation to keep going? It's all about changing the way you think about failure and finding the lessons and opportunities in your setbacks. Here are some tips to help you do that:

⅄ **Shift your mindset.** Instead of seeing failure as a reason to feel bad about yourself or give up, try to see it as a natural part of the learning process. Everyone makes mistakes and faces challenges on their journey to success. By shifting your mindset and seeing failure as an opportunity to learn and grow, you can turn it into motivation to keep going.

⅄ **Learn from your mistakes.** When you experience failure, take some time to reflect on what went wrong and what you can learn from the experience. Maybe you need to try a different approach, practice more, or ask for help from a teacher or mentor. Finding the lessons in your failures can help you avoid making the same mistakes in the future and improve your chances of success.

⅄ **Set new goals.** Instead of dwelling on your failures or getting stuck in a negative mindset, use them as motivation to set new goals and keep moving forward. Think about what you want to achieve and what steps you need to take to get there. Setting new goals gives you something positive to focus on and helps you stay motivated and determined.

⅄ **Stay positive and resilient.** It's important to stay positive and resilient in the face of failure. Instead of letting setbacks drag you down, use them as fuel to keep pushing forward. Focus on the things you can control, like your attitude and effort, and keep taking small steps toward your goals. Remember that setbacks are just temporary roadblocks on the journey to success, and you have the power to overcome them.

▲ **Celebrate your progress.** Even if you haven't reached your ultimate goal yet, take time to celebrate the progress you've made along the way. Every step forward, no matter how small, is worth celebrating. Recognizing your achievements helps you stay motivated and reminds you of how far you've come.

Remember, failure is not the end of the road – it's just a detour on the journey to success. By using failure as motivation to keep going, you can turn setbacks into stepping stones and achieve your goals. So keep pushing forward, keep learning from your mistakes, and keep believing in yourself. You've got this.

Chapter Summary

1. The failure is a natural part of life. Every successful person has experienced failure,

2. Nobody is perfect. We all make mistakes from time to time. So we learn and grow.

3. Asking for suggestion from others meant to help you grow and improve.

4. Seeing failure as a temporary setback as a can help you stay. positive and motivated to keep trying, even when things get tough,

5. By shifting your mindset and seeing failure as an opportunity to learn and grow, you can turn it into motivation to keep going.

9. SURROUNDING YOURSELF WITH SUPPORTIVE PEOPLE

"Surround yourself with only people
who are going to lift you higher"

– Oprah Winfrey

Joining Clubs or Groups That Share Your Interests

Becoming part of a team or community of people who like the same things you do. It's like finding a group of friends who love playing the same games or doing the same activities as you. Here's why joining clubs or groups is important and how you can do it:

First, let's talk about why joining clubs or groups that share your interests is a big deal. When you have hobbies or interests that you're passionate about, it's fun to share them with others who feel the same way. Joining a club or group gives you a chance to meet new friends, learn new things, and have fun doing what you love. It's like finding your tribe – people who understand and appreciate you for who you are.

So how can you join clubs or groups that share your interests? It's easier than you might think! Here are some tips to help you get started:

- **Look for clubs or groups at school.** Many schools have clubs or groups for students who share common interests, like sports teams, art clubs, or science clubs. Check with your school to see what options are available, and consider joining a club that interests you.

- **Ask your friends or classmates.** If you know other kids who share your interests, ask them if they're part of any clubs or groups that you can join. Joining a club with friends can make the experience even more fun and enjoyable.

- **Check out community organizations.** Many communities have clubs or groups for kids who are interested in specific activities or hobbies, like scouting groups, clubs, or youth sports leagues. Look for these organizations in your area and see if any of them appeal to you.

- **Attend club or group meetings or events.** Once you've found a club or group that interests you, attend a meeting or event to see what it's all about. This will give you a chance to meet the other members, learn more about the group's activities, and decide if it's a good fit for you.

- ⚔ **Get involved.** Once you've joined a club or group, get involved and participate in its activities and events. This is a great way to make new friends, learn new skills, and have fun doing what you love. Don't be afraid to share your ideas and contribute to the group in meaningful ways.

- ⚔ **Have fun and be yourself.** Most importantly, have fun and be yourself! Clubs and groups are all about connecting with others who share your interests and enjoying yourself while doing so. So relax, be yourself, and enjoy being part of a community of like-minded individuals.

Remember, joining clubs or groups that share your interests is a great way to make new friends, learn new things, and have fun doing what you love. So don't be afraid to put yourself out there and get involved – you never know what amazing experiences await you.

Attending Community Events or Workshops

Attending community events or workshops means going to gatherings or classes in your neighbourhood where you can learn new things, meet new people, and have fun. It's like going to a big party where you can try out different activities or learn about interesting topics. Here's why attending community events or workshops is important and how you can do it:

First, let's talk about why attending community events or workshops is a big deal. Community events and workshops are a great way to get involved in your neighbourhood, meet new people, and learn new things. They offer a chance to explore your interests, discover new hobbies, and have fun with friends and family. Whether it's a craft fair, a cooking class, or a science workshop, there's something for everyone to enjoy at community events.

Look for events in your neighbourhood. Keep an eye out for posters, flyers, or announcements about upcoming events in your neighbourhood. You can often find information about community events on bulletin boards at local libraries, community centres, or grocery stores. You can also check online for event listings in your area.

Ask your parents or guardians. Your parents or guardians might know about upcoming events in your neighbourhood or be able to help you find information about them. Let them know that you're interested in attending community events or workshops, and ask if they can help you find out more.

Check with local organizations. Many community organizations, like libraries, churches, or recreation centres, host events and workshops for kids and families. Check with these organizations to see if they have any upcoming events that you might be interested in attending.

Invite your friends or family to join you. Attending community events or workshops is even more fun when you go with friends or family. Invite your friends or family members to join you at an event or workshop that interests you, and make a day of it together.

Participate in activities or workshops that interest you. Once you've found a community event or workshop that you'd like to attend, get involved and participate in the activities or workshops that interest you. Whether it's making crafts, learning to cook, or exploring science experiments, there's something for everyone to enjoy at community events.

Have fun and be open to new experiences. Most importantly, have fun and be open to new experiences! Community events and workshops are a great opportunity to try new things, meet new people, and have fun with friends and family. So relax, be yourself, and enjoy all the exciting experiences that your neighbourhood has to offer!

Attending community events or workshops is a great way to get involved in your neighbourhood, meet new people, and learn new things. So don't be afraid to explore your community and take advantage of all the fun and exciting opportunities that are available to you.

Reaching Out to Friends or Family for Support

Talking to the people you care about when you need help, advice, or just someone to talk to. It's like asking your best friend for a hug when you're feeling sad or sharing your excitement with your family when something awesome happens. Here's why reaching out for support is important and how you can do it:

First, let's talk about why reaching out for support is a big deal. When you're facing a challenge or going through a tough time, it can feel overwhelming to deal with it all on your own. That's where friends and family come in – they're there to support you, listen to you, and help you through difficult times. Reaching out for support can help you feel less alone, more understood, and better able to cope with whatever you're going through.

So how can you reach out to friends or family for support? It's easier than you might think! Here are some tips to help you get started:

Talk to someone you trust. When you're feeling sad, stressed, or overwhelmed, reach out to someone you trust and feel comfortable talking to. This could be a friend, a family member, a teacher, or a counsellor – anyone who you know will listen to you without judging you and offer support and understanding.

Be honest about how you're feeling. When you reach out for support, be honest about how you're feeling and what you need. Don't be afraid to share your thoughts, feelings, and concerns with the person you're talking to. Remember, they're there to help you, and they can't do that if they don't know what's going on.

Listen to their advice or perspective. When you reach out for support, be open to listening to the advice or perspective of the person you're talking to. They might have insights or suggestions that you haven't thought of, and their perspective can help you see things in a different light.

Accept their help. When friends or family offer to help you, whether it's by listening to you, offering advice, or just being there for you, accept their help graciously. Remember that it's okay to lean on others for support when you need it, and that accepting help doesn't make you weak – it makes you human.

Express gratitude. After reaching out for support and receiving help from friends or family, be sure to express your gratitude and appreciation. Let them know how much their support means to you and how grateful you are to have them in your life.

Reaching out to friends or family for support is a sign of strength, not weakness. It shows that you're willing to ask for help when you need it and that you understand the importance of connection and support in difficult times. So don't be afraid to reach out – you're not alone, and there are people who care about you and want to help you through whatever you're going through.

Finding a Mentor or Role Model

Looking up to someone who inspires you, teaches you, and helps you grow. It's like having a superhero or a wise owl to guide you on your journey through life. Here's why finding a mentor or role model is important and how you can do it: First, let's talk about why finding a mentor or role model is a big deal. When you have someone to look up to and learn from, it can make a big difference in your life. A mentor or role model can inspire you to be your best self, encourage you to pursue your dreams, and offer guidance and support when you need it. They're like a guiding star that helps you navigate the ups and downs of life.

So how can you find a mentor or role model? It's easier than you might think! Here are some tips to help you get started:

Look for someone you admire. Think about people in your life – family members, teachers, coaches, or community leaders – who you admire and respect. What is it about them that you admire? Maybe it's their kindness, their determination, or their ability to make others laugh. Finding someone you admire is the first step to finding a mentor or role model.

Reach out to them. Once you've identified someone you admire, don't be afraid to reach out to them and let them know. You can start by telling them how much you admire them and why. You can also ask if they'd be willing to mentor you or if you can learn from them in some way. Most people are flattered to be asked and happy to help others learn and grow.

Learn from their example. Once you've found a mentor or role model, pay attention to their actions, words, and behaviours. What can you learn from them? Maybe they have a positive attitude, a strong work ethic, or a knack for solving problems. By observing and learning from their example, you can develop your own skills and qualities.

Ask for advice or guidance. Don't be afraid to ask your mentor or role model for advice or guidance when you need it. Whether you're facing a difficult decision, struggling with a problem, or just need someone to talk to, your mentor or role model can offer valuable insights and support.

Be open to feedback. When your mentor or role model offers feedback or suggestions, be open to receiving it. Remember that they have your best interests at heart and are trying to help you become the best version of yourself. Listen to what they have to say, consider their advice carefully, and be willing to make changes or improvements based on their feedback.

Remember, finding a mentor or role model can have a big impact on your life. They can inspire you, teach you, and help you grow in ways you never imagined. So don't be afraid to reach out and find someone who can guide you on your journey. You never know – you might just find a lifelong friend and mentor who will be by your side every step of the way.

Building a Support Network of Like-Minded Individuals

Surrounding yourself with people who share your interests, values, and goals. It's like creating a team of friends who understand and support you in everything you do. Here's why building a support network is important and how you can do it: First, let's talk about why building a support network is a big deal. When you have a group of like-minded individuals to lean on, it can make a big difference in your life. These are the people who get you, who cheer you on, and who are there for you when you need a helping hand or a listening ear. Building a support network can help you feel less alone, more understood, and more confident in yourself and your abilities.

So how can you build a support network of like-minded individuals? It's easier than you might think! Here are some tips to help you get started:

Find people who share your interests. Think about the things you love to do – whether it's playing sports, making art, reading books, or exploring nature – and look for people who share those interests. You can find like-minded individuals in clubs, classes, teams, or online communities dedicated to your favourite activities.

Be open to making new friends. Building a support network starts with making connections with others. Be open to meeting new people and getting to know them. Strike up conversations, ask questions, and be friendly and approachable. You never know – your next best friend or biggest supporter could be just around the corner.

Seek out opportunities to connect. Look for opportunities to connect with like-minded individuals in your community or online. Attend events, join clubs or groups, participate in classes or workshops, or join online forums or social media groups dedicated to your interests. These are all great ways to meet new people who share your passions and values.

Be supportive of others. Building a support network is a two-way street. Just as you want others to support you, be sure to offer your support to them as well. Celebrate their successes, lend a listening ear when they need to talk, and offer a helping hand whenever you can. By being supportive of others, you'll build strong and meaningful connections that last a lifetime.

Nurture your relationships. Once you've found like-minded individuals to connect with, take the time to nurture and strengthen your relationships with them. Make an effort to stay in touch, spend time together, and show them that you care. Building a support network is about more than just making connections – it's about cultivating meaningful relationships that enrich your life.

Remember, building a support network of like-minded individuals is an important part of living a happy and fulfilling life. These are the people who lift you up, inspire you, and help you become the best version of yourself. So don't be afraid to reach out and make connections with others who share your interests and values. You'll be glad you did.

Chapter Summary

1. Surround yourself likeminded people enjoy being part of a communities.

2. Community events and workshops are a great opportunity to try new thing, meet new people, and here fun with friends and family.

3. Reaching out to friends or family for support is a sign of strength, not weakness.

4. A mentor or role model can inspire you to be best yourself, encourage you to pursue your dreams, and offer guidance and support when you neet it.

5. Building a support network of like-minded individuals is an important part of living a happy and fulfilling life.

10. BECOMING YOUR BEST SELF

"The journey of a thousand
miles begins with one step"

— Lao Tzu

Setting Intentions for Future Growth

Setting intentions for future growth means making plans and goals for how you want to improve and develop as a person. It's like planting seeds in a garden and taking care of them so they can grow into strong and healthy plants. Here's why setting intentions are important and how you can do it:

First, let's talk about why setting intentions for future growth is a big deal. When you have a clear idea of what you want to achieve and how you want to grow, it can help you stay focused, motivated, and on track. Setting intentions gives you a sense of purpose and direction, and it empowers you to take control of your own growth and development.

So how can you set intentions for future growth? It's easier than you might think! Here are some tips to help you get started:

- ▲ **Reflect on your strengths and areas for improvement.** Think about the things you're good at and the things you'd like to get better at. Maybe you're a great artist but struggle with math, or maybe you're a star athlete but could use some help with time management. Reflecting on your strengths and areas for improvement can help you identify areas where you want to grow.

- ▲ **Set specific, achievable goals.** Once you've identified areas for growth, set specific goals for how you want to improve. Make sure your goals are realistic and achievable, and break them down into smaller, manageable steps. For example, if you want to improve your math skills, your goal might be to practice multiplication tables for 10 minutes every day.

- ▲ **Write down your intentions.** Writing down your intentions can help solidify them in your mind and make them feel more real and tangible. Take some time to write down your goals and intentions for future growth, and keep them somewhere where you can see them regularly, like on a poster on your wall or in a notebook.

⋏ **Create a plan of action.** Once you've set your intentions and goals, create a plan of action for how you're going to achieve them. Break down your goals into smaller, actionable steps, and set deadlines for when you want to accomplish each step. Having a plan in place can help you stay organized and focused on your goals.

⋏ **Stay committed and flexible.** Achieving your goals and intentions for future growth takes time and effort, so stay committed to your plan even when things get tough. Be willing to adjust your plan if needed and stay flexible in the face of challenges or setbacks. Remember, it's okay to make mistakes or change course along the way – what's important is that you keep moving forward.

⋏ **Celebrate your progress.** As you work towards your goals and intentions, take time to celebrate your progress along the way. Whether it's reaching a milestone, mastering a new skill, or overcoming a challenge, celebrate your achievements and give yourself a pat on the back for all your hard work.

Setting intentions for future growth is all about taking control of your own development and striving to become the best version of yourself. By reflecting on your strengths and areas for improvement, setting specific goals, creating a plan of action, staying committed and flexible, and celebrating your progress, you can achieve great things and reach your full potential. So go ahead — set your intentions for future growth and watch yourself bloom and grow.

Reflecting on Your Personal Growth Journey

Looking back on the changes and progress you've made as a person over time. It's like flipping through the pages of a photo album and seeing how much you've grown and changed from year to year. Here's why reflecting on your personal growth journey is important and how you can do it:

First, let's talk about why reflecting on your personal growth journey is a big deal. When you take the time to reflect on how far you've come and the challenges you've overcome, it can help you feel proud of yourself and more confident in your abilities. Reflecting on your personal growth journey also gives you insights into what has helped you grow and develop as a person, which can be valuable information for your future growth and development.

So how can you reflect on your personal growth journey? It's easier than you might think! Here are some tips to help you get started:

Take a trip down memory lane. Set aside some time to think back on your life and the experiences you've had. You can start by looking through old photos, journals, or keepsakes that remind you of important moments in your life. As you reminisce, think about how these experiences have shaped you into the person you are today.

Consider your achievements and milestones. Think about the things you've accomplished and the milestones you've reached over the years. These could be big things, like winning an award or graduating from school, or smaller things, like learning to ride a bike or making a new friend. Reflecting on your achievements can help you feel proud of yourself and motivated to keep growing and reaching for your goals.

Think about your challenges and setbacks. Reflecting on your personal growth journey isn't just about celebrating your successes – it's also about acknowledging the challenges and setbacks you've faced along the way. Think about the times when things didn't go as planned or when you felt like giving up. How did you overcome these challenges? What did you learn from them? Reflecting on your challenges can help you see how resilient and capable you are, even in the face of adversity.

Consider your values and beliefs. Reflecting on your personal growth journey also involves thinking about your values and beliefs and how they have evolved over time. What are the things that are most important to you? How have your values and beliefs influenced the decisions you've made and the person you've become? Reflecting on your values and beliefs can help you better understand yourself and what drives you.

Write down your reflections. Once you've spent some time reflecting on your personal growth journey, consider writing down your thoughts and reflections in a journal or notebook. Writing can help you organize your thoughts and feelings and make sense of your experiences. You can also use your reflections to set goals for your future growth and development.

Reflecting on your personal growth journey is an important part of learning and growing as a person. By taking the time to look back on your experiences, achievements, challenges, values, and beliefs, you can gain valuable insights into yourself and your journey through life. So take a moment to reflect on how far you've come and all that you've accomplished – you might just surprise yourself with how much you've grown.

Continuing to Challenge Yourself

Pushing you to try new things, learn new skills, and overcome obstacles, even when it's hard. It's like climbing a mountain – each new challenge you tackle helps you grow stronger and more confident. Here's why continuing to challenge yourself is important and how you can do it:

First, let's talk about why continuing to challenge you is a big deal. When you step out of your comfort zone and take on new challenges, you build confidence in yourself and your abilities. You also expand your skills and knowledge, which can open up new opportunities and help you reach your goals. Challenging yourself keeps life exciting and rewarding, and it helps you become the best version of yourself.

So how can you continue to challenge yourself? It's easier than you might think! Here are some tips to help you get started:

Try new things. One of the best ways to challenge yourself is to try new things that you've never done before. This could be anything from learning to play a musical instrument, trying a new sport, or taking up a new hobby. Stepping out of your comfort zone and trying new things can be scary, but it can also be incredibly rewarding and fun.

Set goals for yourself. Another way to challenge yourself is to set goals for what you want to achieve. Your goals could be big or small, short-term or long-term – the important thing is that they push you to stretch yourself and grow. Whether it's getting better at math, making new friends, or running a marathon, setting goals gives you something to work towards and motivates you to keep pushing yourself.

Take on challenges. Look for opportunities to challenge yourself in different areas of your life. This could be anything from taking on a challenging school project, volunteering for a leadership role, or participating in a competition or event. Taking on challenges helps you build resilience, perseverance, and problem-solving skills, which are important qualities for success in school and beyond.

Embrace failure as a learning opportunity. When you're challenging yourself, it's inevitable that you'll encounter obstacles and setbacks along the way. Instead of letting failure discourage you, see it as a chance to learn and grow.

Reflect on what went wrong, what you can do differently next time, and how you can use the experience to become stronger and more resilient.

Celebrate your successes. As you continue to challenge yourself and achieve your goals, take time to celebrate your successes and accomplishments. Whether it's reaching a milestone, overcoming a difficult obstacle, or mastering a new skill, celebrating your successes boosts your confidence and motivates you to keep challenging yourself in the future.

Continuing to challenge you is an important part of personal growth and development. By stepping out of your comfort zone, setting goals, taking on challenges, embracing failure, and celebrating your successes, you can become the best version of yourself and achieve great things. So don't be afraid to challenge yourself – you never know what amazing things you might accomplish.

Expressing Gratitude for Your Progress

Taking the time to appreciate and be thankful for the growth and achievements you've made in your life. It's like saying thank you for all the good things that have happened to you and acknowledging the effort you've put into becoming the person you are today. Here's why expressing gratitude for your progress is important and how you can do it:

First, let's talk about why expressing gratitude for your progress is a big deal. When you take the time to recognize and be thankful for the progress you've made, it helps you feel happier, more fulfilled, and more positive about yourself and your life. Expressing gratitude also helps you stay motivated and focused on your goals, and it strengthens your relationships with others by showing them that you appreciate their support and encouragement.

So how can you express gratitude for your progress? It's easier than you might think! Here are some tips to help you get started:

Take time to reflect on your progress. Set aside some time each day or week to reflect on the progress you've made in different areas of your life. Think about the goals you've achieved, the obstacles you've overcome, and the positive changes you've noticed in yourself. Reflecting on your progress helps you appreciate how far you've come and motivates you to keep moving forward.

Keep a gratitude journal. One way to express gratitude for your progress is to keep a gratitude journal where you write down things you're thankful for each day. Take a few minutes before bed to jot down three things you're grateful for, whether it's a kind gesture from a friend, a small victory at school, or a beautiful sunset. Keeping a gratitude journal helps you focus on the positive things in your life and cultivate a mindset of gratitude.

Say thank you to others. Another way to express gratitude for your progress is to say thank you to the people who have supported and encouraged you along the way. Whether it's your parents, teachers, friends, or coaches, take the time to thank them for their help, guidance, and encouragement. A simple thank you can go a long way in showing others how much you appreciate them and their support.

Celebrate your achievements. When you achieve a goal or reach a milestone, take time to celebrate your achievements and acknowledge your hard work and dedication. Whether it's treating yourself to a special meal, doing something fun with friends, or simply giving yourself a pat on the back, celebrating your achievements boosts your confidence and motivates you to keep striving for success.

Pay it forward. Finally, one of the best ways to express gratitude for your progress is to pay it forward and help others who are on their own journey of growth and development. Whether it's offering a word of encouragement, sharing your experiences and insights, or lending a helping hand, helping others is a powerful way to express gratitude and make a positive impact in the world.

Expressing gratitude for your progress is an important part of personal growth and development. By taking the time to reflect on your progress, keep a gratitude journal, say thank you to others, celebrate your achievements, and pay it forward, you can cultivate a mindset of gratitude and appreciation that enriches your life and the lives of those around you. So take a moment to express gratitude for your progress – you'll be glad you did.

Sharing Your Journey with Others to Inspire Them

Telling people about your experiences, challenges, and successes in a way that motivates and encourages them to pursue their own goals and dreams. It's like being a storyteller who shares their adventures to inspire others to embark on their own journeys of growth and discovery. Here's why sharing your journey is important and how you can do it:

First, let's talk about why sharing your journey with others to inspire them is a big deal. When you share your experiences and successes with others, it shows them that they're not alone in their struggles and challenges. It also gives them hope and motivation to overcome obstacles and pursue their own goals and dreams. Sharing your journey can be a powerful way to make a positive impact in the lives of others and inspire them to believe in themselves and their abilities.

So how can you share your journey with others to inspire them? It's easier than you might think! Here are some tips to help you get started:

Be authentic and honest. When sharing your journey with others, be authentic and honest about your experiences, both the good and the bad. People are more likely to be inspired by your story if they can relate to your struggles and challenges. Be open about the obstacles you've faced and the lessons you've learned along the way.

Focus on the positive. While it's important to be honest about your challenges, try to focus on the positive aspects of your journey as well. Highlight your successes, achievements, and moments of growth and transformation. By sharing the positive aspects of your journey, you can inspire others to believe in themselves and their ability to overcome obstacles.

Use storytelling techniques. One of the most effective ways to share your journey with others is through storytelling. Use descriptive language, vivid imagery, and personal anecdotes to bring your experiences to life and make them relatable and engaging. Share specific examples and stories that illustrate the lessons you've learned and the growth you've experienced.

Show empathy and understanding. When sharing your journey with others, show empathy and understanding for their own struggles and challenges. Acknowledge that everyone's journey is unique and that it's okay to face setbacks and obstacles along the way. Offer words of encouragement and support, and let them know that you believe in their ability to succeed.

Lead by example. Finally, one of the best ways to inspire others is to lead by example and live your life in a way that reflects your values and beliefs. Be proactive in pursuing your goals and dreams, and don't be afraid to take risks and step out of your comfort zone. By living authentically and passionately, you can inspire others to do the same and pursue their own dreams with courage and determination.

Sharing your journey with others to inspire them is a powerful way to make a positive impact in the world. By being authentic and honest, focusing on the positive, using storytelling techniques, showing empathy and understanding, and leading by example, you can inspire others to believe in themselves and pursue their own goals and dreams. So don't be afraid to share your journey – you never know who you might inspire along the way.

Chapter Summary

1. Setting intentions of future. Growth is all about taking control of your own development and striving to become the best version of yourself.

2. Reflecting on your personal growth Journey is an important part of learning and growing as a person.

3. One of the best ways to challenge yourself is try new things that you've never done before.

4. Keeping a gratitude journal helps you focus on the positive things in your life and cultivate a mindset of gratitude.

5. Sharing your journey with others to inspire them is a big deal.

CONCLUSION

Staying motivated for a long time can be challenging, but it is possible when you ignite your passion. Passion is what keeps you excited and eager to continue, even when things are tough. To find and keep your passion, remember these important steps.

First, find what you love. Think about the activities that make you happy and excited. These are clues to your passions. When you do something you love, it doesn't feel like work. It feels fun and rewarding. Try different activities to discover what you truly enjoy.

Once you find your passion, set goals. Goals give you something to aim for and keep you focused. They can be small, like practicing for 15 minutes a day, or big, like writing a book. Achieving goals gives you a sense of accomplishment and keeps you motivated.

Another way to keep your passion alive is to keep learning and improving. When you get better at something, you feel more confident and proud. Take classes, read books, and practice regularly. Don't be afraid to make mistakes because they help you learn. The more you know, the more exciting your passion becomes.

Surround yourself with supportive people. Friends, family, and mentors who encourage you can make a big difference. They can cheer you on and give you advice. Join clubs or groups where you can meet others who share your passion. Being part of a community makes the journey more enjoyable.

It's normal to feel tired or frustrated sometimes, even when you are passionate about something. When this happens, take a break and relax. Rest helps you recharge your energy. Remember why you started and think about the joy your passion brings you. This helps you stay motivated during tough times.

Celebrate your achievements, no matter how small. Recognizing your progress boosts your confidence and keeps you motivated. Reward yourself for reaching your goals and share your successes with others. Celebrating makes the journey fun and reminds you of how far you've come.

In summary, the secret to enduring motivation is to ignite your passion. Find what you love, set goals, keep learning, surround yourself with support, take breaks when needed, and celebrate your achievements. Following these steps makes it easier to stay excited and motivated, no matter what challenges you face. Passion is the fuel that keeps you going, so keep it alive and enjoy the journey.

CASE STUDY

Initial Struggles

Jan 2010 - Kumar faces a lack of motivation and struggles to find purpose in his daily tasks.

Discovering Passion

Mar - 2010 Kumar attends a workshop and discovers his passion for graphic design, igniting a spark of motivation.

Setting Goals

Jun 2010 - Kumar sets clear, achievable goals to improve his skills and advance his career in graphic design.

Building a Routine

Sep 2010 - Kumar establishes a daily routine that includes dedicated time for learning and practice.

Seeking Mentorship

Dec 2010 -Kumar finds a mentor who provides guidance, feedback, and encouragement, boosting his motivation.

Overcoming Setbacks

Mar 2011- Kumar faces and overcomes several setbacks, learning resilience and maintaining his drive.

Achieving Milestones

Jun 2011 - Kumar achieves significant milestones, including his first freelance project and a portfolio showcase.

Sustaining Motivation

Dec 2011 - Kumar continues to set new goals and seek inspiration, sustaining his motivation over the long term.